Pokemon Go Game Guide Unofficial

Copyright 2016 by TheYuw
Third Edition, License Notes

Presented by HiddenStuffEntertainment.com

Table of Contents

Preface

We want to take a moment to say thank you for purchasing our strategy guide online. HiddenStuff Entertainment remains one of the top app and eBook publishers online. It is our commitment to bring you the latest support and strategies for today's most popular games.

We sincerely hope that you find this guide useful and beneficial in your quest for digital immortality. We want to provide gamers with knowledge and build their skills to perform at the highest levels within their games. This in turn contributes to a positive and more enjoyable experience. After all, it is our belief that things in life are to be enjoyed as much as they possibly can be.

If you game on a regular basis and are involved in some of the top titles online, we wanted to extend a special offer to gain access to free resources provided exclusively by us.

As an added bonus to your purchase please follow the "CLICK HERE" link below to sign-up for our free eBooks and guides program. Here you will receive free guides and resources for today's most popular games, mobile apps, and devices! Sing-up for free below. It's our way of saying thanks for being a valued customer!

CLICK HERE TO SIGN-UP FOR FREE

How to Install the Game for the Kindle

1) Start your Kindle Device.

2) On the main screen click: "Apps".

3) Click: "Store".

4) Search the App name in the top search box.

5) Click on the "Free/Download" button and wait for the app to install on your device.

6) Locate the installed application by clicking: "Library". Click on the icon to begin playing. Enjoy!

How to Install the Game for the iPad/iPhone

1) Locate the IOS App Store Icon on your phone/tablet and click on it.

2) Type the name of the game in the IOS search box.

3) Click on the "Install" Icon within the application's page.

4) Once it has finished installing locate it on your device and click it to begin playing.

How to Install the Game for Android Devices

1) Locate the Google Play App Store Icon on your phone/tablet and click on it.

2) Click on the Magnifying Glass Search Icon located in the top right of the screen.

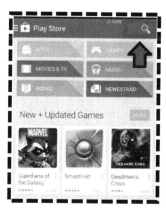

3) Search the game name that you want to download.
4) Click on the "Install" icon.

5) Once the game has installed. Find the game icon on your device and click it to begin playing. Enjoy!

How to Install for Windows Phone

1) Locate the Windows Phone App Store Icon on your phone/tablet and click on it.

2) Click on the Magnifying Glass Search Icon located in the bottom middle of the screen.

3) Click on the "Install" icon.

4) Once the game has installed. Find the game icon on your device and click it to begin playing. Enjoy!

How to Install for Windows 8

1) Locate the Windows Phone App Store Icon on your phone/tablet and click on it.

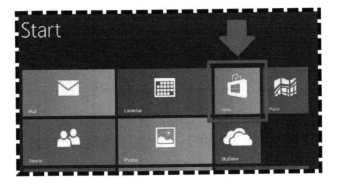

2) Locate the Search box and search for the app that you want to download.

3) Click on the Download Icon to download and install the app.

4) Once the game has installed. Find the game icon on your device and click it to begin playing. Enjoy!

How to Install for Blackberry

1) Locate the Blackberry App Store Icon on your phone/tablet and click on it.

2) Locate the Search box and enter the name of the app you want to download.

3) Click the Download icon to download and install the app.

How to Install for Nook

1) Locate the Nook App Store Icon on your phone/tablet and click on it.

2) Locate the Search box and enter the name of the app you want to download.

3) Click the Install button to download and install the app.

4) Open the app on the main screen of the device.

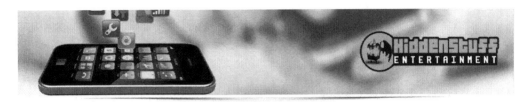

How to Install the Game on your PC

1) Go to Google and search "facebook app games" by typing it into the search bar.

2) Click on the second search result labeled: "Games – Facebook".

3) In the right hand side search bar type in the name of the game you want to download.

4) Click the "Play Now" button to begin playing. Enjoy!

Introduction

Pokémon GO is a new mobile game released in July, 2016. Every Pokémon lover in the world will definitely download the game, and the competition you will have in being the best Pokémon master s quite big. That is why this guide is here to help you!

You've just started Charmander is in your living room, and you already know that you will spend so much time playing this game. But, what else can you do?

Basically, it's a traditional Pokémon hunting. But Pokémon GO, unlike other games you might find, is new, modern version of a game which is jet to be developed completely. We are here to help you catch 'em all!

Basics

Setup

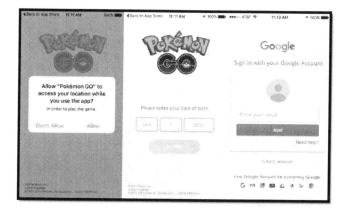

When you download the app, you need to register. Set your birth date. Then you need to choose if you are going to log into through Pokémon Trainer Club or Google. We recommend using Google (unless you already have account into Trainer Club). You also need to give the game permission to access your location. You'll learn why soon enough.

Customize your character

First thing you are choosing if, of course, the gender. After you've chosen the gender, it is time to customize your character. You can choose skin color, eye color and hair color, and then you have clothes to choose from.

After you are done customizing your character, Professor Willow will introduce to you. After that you will get your first Poke Balls and start the game!

How to find a Pokémon?

This one is probably one of the coolest features in this game! Now you can learn the reason why you need to give your GPS location. It downloads the real data and will place you onto your real location. To begin with, this will help you find a Pokémon.

A Pokémon can be find anywhere, just as it could be in the real life. More of them will outside, but don't be surprised if you find one in your kitchen, too. How to find it?

When you notice little shags of leaves whirling, that is where the Pokémon is hiding! The grass animations are here with purpose, and that is to help you catch the Pokemon. The circle around your character will tell you how close you need to be if you want to catch that Pokémon. He needs to be inside the circle. When he is, tap on him to capture it.

Capturing Pokémon

So you've find Pokémon, you clicked on it. Now, capture it. Be careful and don't rush, since you have definite number of Poké Balls.

Hold down the Ball with your fingertip. The green circle will show around the Pokémon. While the green circle is largest, hit the Pokémon with the ball. Have you succeed?

But be careful, it is not finished. Perhaps your Pokémon won't stay in the Poke Ball. The ball will rumble a few times and if you succeeded, you will get the stars. If not, the Pokémon will appear again. Notice that you can see how hard wll it be to capture a Pokémon by the color of its circle.

The Pokémon with green colored circle are easiest one to catch, but Pokémon that is harder to capture will bring you a higher boost. So try both.

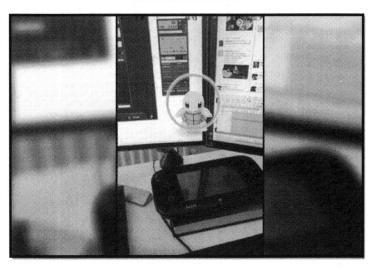

Poké Stops

PokeStops are places where you can get a free stuff, including poke balls, when you stop there. You will recognize PokeStop by a blue square on the map.

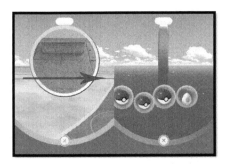

Tips & Strategies

Do not rush

You can train your Pokémon on some places. They look as the one on the photo right.

You still can't battle in the real life, but you can always go to the gym and train.

Be patient. You need to be level 5 to battle, and you level up by earning experience points. So far no one made it to this level, and that is why you need to be patient.

Remember that Pokémon Go is a new game that is jet to be modified. The chances of you being kicked out of the app from time to time are huge, but don't let that frustrate you too much. Developers are working on the game every day.

Now when you've learned the basis, here are some extra tips:

Exeggcute was caught!

While capturing a Pokémon, try drawing a small circle around Poke Ball. You will get a nice curve and some bonus points.

You can also hold on the Pokéball. Now, make a rotating motion. When it sparkles, let the ball fly. Don't be discouraged if this doesn't succeed when you try it the first time. With a little practice you'll learn how to master the skill.

How close is Pokemon to you?

You can see paw prints on the photo. The Pokémon's with one paw are close to you.

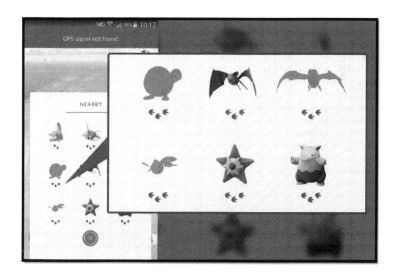

Don't waste your pokeball!

Tap and hold! This will bring a green circle about the Pokémon, and you know what to do next.

Here is the example of the Pokémon with yellow circle. This one is harder to catch.

How to increase your chances of capturing?

Once you are higher level, you will get Razz Berries to feed Pokémon and make them easier to catch. You will get Razz Berries when you stop at Poke Stops.

Incense

Christian Zamora @Christian_Zamo · Jul 7
~And while I wait, I put on my perfume~

Yes, you can use an incense to help you! This will help you
get more Pokémons near you. You will get two of them at the
beginning of your game.

Lure Module

Go to a Poke Stop and purchase this item. As you can see, it attracts Pokémon to a PokeStop for 30 minutes.

Transfer duplicates to the Professor

You will get a few of the same kind throughout the game, and you won't need all of them. That is why you have an option to transfer duplicated Pokemon to the proffesor.

Pokéball button –> left icon -> pick a Pokémon and scroll down –> "Transfer"

When you transfer Pokemon to professor, you get a candy.

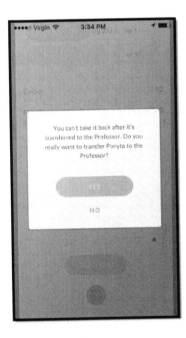

Incubate the eggs

Put an egg in an incubator. You have one in your backpack. Now you should wait, because the egg would eventually hatch and you'll get new Pokémon, a candy, or some other reward.

The bigger the egg, the better the reward.

1.42/5 km

Walk to hatch this Egg.

Find a Pokemon of a certain type near their habitat

For instance, water-typed Pokémon are more likely to be near a see, river or a lake, etc.

Turn off the camera (optional)

The animated version still looks better than the real life one, and while you are catching the Pokémon you can turn off the camera to get this animated version.

A battery saver

The main menu -> Settings

Of course, this game drains a lot of battery. Just turn on the battery saver to save it a bit.

Daily free items

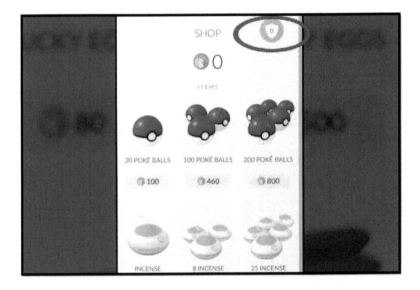

If there isn't a shop nearby, click on the Shop menu on the
Pokeball icon. Now, to the top right you will notice the
'shield' icon. Tap it for a daily bonus.

If you want to hatch an egg, leave the app open

Meowth / CP 101

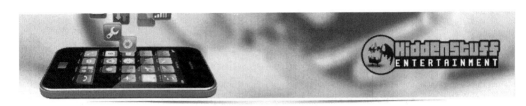

When your phone is a sleep, nothing happens. Hence, if you want to hatch an egg (for what you need to walk a certain distance) you need to leave an app open.

Give your Pokemon a full health bar

Your Pokémon might get knocked out. Evolving a Pokémon that has no health (knocked out Pokemon) would bring it back with full health.

How to catch a Pokemon while standing still?

By standing still, you will be able to see any Pokémon within a short radius. We recommend you walk about a 100 meters and then just stand still. Random Pokémons will show up.

How to name a Pokemon?

The photo you see on the left is pretty self-explanatory.
Pokemon menu -> pick a monster and tap on the tiny pencil

A special moves in the battle

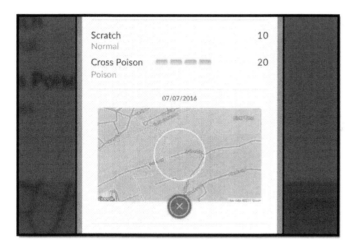

We've mentioned earlier that you can't battle in the real time jet, but you can fight in the gym as training. When you just start doing so, it will be hard, since you might fight with more skilled players. But don't worry. You still have a chance to win at the last second.

Recovering a data

As we already said, the game is not perfect jet and it has a few bugs. Let's hope this won't happen, but chances are all your progress might get wiped.

Don't worry.

First, find a way to close Pokémon GO. After you've closed the app, re-open it to get the fresh connection to the server. This is probably going to restore your data.

Conclusion

Once you start to implement the strategies outlined there will be a much greater chance of success for you. In addition, you will find yourself beating parts of the game that you were once stuck on. This will not only make the game much more interesting and enjoyable but you will also realize a greater level of accomplishment. Good luck!

Free Bonus for our Readers

Thank-you for purchasing our eBook. We hope that in these readings you will have found value and helpful information. As an added bonus to your purchase please follow the "CLICK HERE" link below to sign-up for our free eBooks and guides program. Here you will receive free guides and resources for today's most popular games, mobile apps, and devices!

This is an exclusive and private offer for our customers. There is no purchase required, its 100% secure, and we will not send spam email of any kind. Just relevant strategies for today's most popular titles! To get started you can sing-up for free below.

CLICK HERE TO CLAIM YOUR FREE BONUS

54019280R00034

Made in the USA
Lexington, KY
29 July 2016